The Fruit of Life

For Terri

The Fruit of Life

A Collection of Christian Poetic Tales

William "Bill" C. Scheel II

Sheffield Publishing House
New York, NY
www.sheffieldpublishinghouse.com

Table of Contents

Introduction

By William C. Scheel II

When I started writing poetry, the thought of having my poems published seemed only a distant goal. I wrote infrequently and usually after an event that had strongly impacted me.

In 2011, my wife, Terri, and I started going to a different church. I was moved by the insightful perspective of a particular teacher; I realized that my walk as a Christian had not been fruitful enough. I wasn't being obedient to God. I believe the Holy Spirit was impressing upon me that I had this gift of writing poetry but wasn't using it. When I repented and surrendered my whole life to the work of Christ, the full power and inspiration of these poems came into being. I started writing in earnest in February of 2011 and completed the final poem, "Relief Is Belief," in March of 2012. My prayer was that my finish would be strong and that my legacy as God's vessel would spread the message of the "good news" there is in Jesus Christ.

2 | *Foreword*

Foreword

By Terri Scheel

When Bill asked me to write a foreword about the poems he has written in our poetry book, I thought I would write about witnessing the inspiration and the motivation Bill had when writing his poetry. We believe the spirit of the Lord inspired these writings, leaving us with the inalienable knowledge that they have great purpose in the Kingdom of God. Bill would be impressed by a theme. Shortly afterward, he would begin his poem and would usually complete it in a couple of hours. To me, his writings are a perfect "One Way" sign pointing toward Jesus Christ.

I am honored to have been a part of the poems' infancies. Bill would often share his latest poem with me, and I would be astonished by the depth and insight. Those who read these poems will enjoy verbal surprises and will constantly anticipate the next stanza of lyric that changes their perspective with profound significance.

* * *

By Charles Sheffield

When Bill asked me—well, actually told me—to write a foreword for his book, I thought, "My gosh, there's so much to say about Bill. How can I condense what could be enough material for a book into a foreword?" As a couple of fifteen year olds, Bill and I met in tenth-grade homeroom class. We became fast friends, and although we took different paths after high school and saw less of each other, we still remained good friends.

In early 1984, I decided to expand my construction business and started Gulf Coast Fan and Light, Inc. to provide and install ceiling fans to the home-building market. My friend Bill was the first person I thought of. I called and asked him to join me in the company. Bill was an electrician, and I wanted him to take care of the fan installation. After thinking about it for about thirty seconds, he enthusiastically shouted, "Yes!" So, with Bill as our installer and Susan Gerk as our customer service person, we hired an outside salesperson and began operations.

After four months in business, it became apparent that our outside salesperson wasn't up to the task. I called Bill into my office and told him that I needed him to take over sales. He was a bit hesitant since he was an electrician and had never been involved in sales. So, to convince him, I put it in terms he could understand. I told him that I needed someone that I could trust to be honest with and to take care of the customers and that if he didn't take the position, I would shut the business down. His immediate reply was, "I'll do it!" The rest is history.

For the next two months, Bill came into my office several times a day and tried to sell me ceiling fans. As a national general contractor without much free time on my hands, I had no patience for salespeople who wasted my time with irrelevant details or products that didn't provide greater value. I was unmerciful on the inexperienced salesman Bill. My goal was to be the toughest, meanest, and nastiest customer that he would ever come across. On some occasions, I would just be extremely blunt and tell him that he was wasting my time. Other times, I would yell at him, get red-faced, and tell him to get out of my office. Most people would have told me where to go and stormed out. Not Bill. He never lost his cool and would come right back with a smile on his face and the determination to see things from the customer's perspective. And he did.

Over the next twenty-eight years, Bill dedicated his life to helping create an organization built around solving the customers' problems by providing them with the best service and products available. Bill the electrician helped create and put into action the installation procedures that became a cornerstone of the success of Gulf Coast Fan and Light, Inc. Bill the armchair engineer provided invaluable input into making our Old Jacksonville Ceiling Fans one of the most reliable, quietest, smoothest, and easiest-to-install fans on the market. Bill the preacher always made sure the employees knew our customers' needs and the importance of satisfying those needs to the highest-possible degree. Bill truly became the customers' advocate.

The above tells of Bill's business accomplishments. Now I would like to tell you a bit about Bill the man. By focusing on his qualities and using his writing medium of poetry, I hope to provide a clearer picture of Bill.

My Friend Bill . . .

He is my friend extraordinaire.
When needed, he is always there.
That he is a great guy is undeniable,
For his character is among the most reliable.

My friend Bill is loyal to a fault.
He provides the type friendship that is forever sought.
To him his friends shall always be bound.
He is so great to have around.

My friend Bill, with his heart of gold,
The kindness of his spirit always bold,
In his endeavors is straightforward and sincere.
The place he holds for his fellow man is so dear.

My friend Bill is a loving husband and father.
Whatever his family needs is never a bother.
His wife, he refers to as his beautiful bride.
For him, his family is always a source of pride.

My friend Bill is a man of God.
Upon his fellow man, he does not trod.
For in his character, integrity is a must,
And so to him, we all place our trust.

My friend Bill, to be the customers' advocate is his mission.
For this result, he sees his task through to fruition.
Diligent and conscientious as he moves forward,
Our customers' deep satisfaction is his just reward.

My friend Bill, to our employees a great example he did set
With the high ideals and achievements he has met.
In the wake of his light, which so brightly shone,
His legacy in our company is as cast of stone.

My friend Bill, you have passed and are no longer here.
But everything in me says that you are still near.
For you were always larger than life in essence,
It is so strongly that I continue to feel your presence.

I shall miss you so, Bill, my dear friend.
You remained strong and faithful to the end.
Although your body became withered and weak,
Your mind, heart, and sprit were always at a peak.

You are truly an inspiration to us all,
A man among men who stood tall.
My friend Bill still fills us all with his love
As if he is saying, as he looks down from above,

"My time here is done, and now I must go.
The rest of you, cry no tears and get on with the show!"
"Go out and celebrate life with lots of fun stuff,
For life is short and I shall be seeing you soon enough."

By Charles Sheffield
Written in fond memory of and in tribute to Bill Scheel (August 29,1954, to March 8, 2012). This poem was began on February 27, 2012, and was completed postmortem on March 12, 2012.

* * *

By John Boucher

I was honored when Bill Scheel asked me to write a foreword for his book. Bill is to be commended for his outstanding contributions to the ceiling fan business during the more than twenty-five years of his management career. Bill came into my life in the late 1980s as the head of sales for Gulf Coast Fan and Light and its affiliate company, Old Jacksonville Ceiling Fan Company. When I met Bill, I was a partner in the fan-manufacturing business Chien Luen Industries Inc./King of Fans and was responsible for creating new fan designs, new technology, and new business development. We manufactured fans for most of the big brands, including Hunter, Monte Carlo, Emerson, Casa Blanca, and a number of others. Over the years, we produced approximately 50 million fans in over 4,000 different designs.

When we partnered with Gulf Coast Fan and Light in the manufacture of the Old Jacksonville Ceiling Fan, we gained access to the vast knowledge of Bill Scheel and the Gulf Coast Fan and Light team. Gulf Coast Fan and Light, one of the largest—if not the largest—ceiling fan installation companies in the United States provided us with feedback that had previously been unavailable through our retailing customers due to their lack of understanding of the problems faced by the homeowners purchasing the fans. The feedback we had been receiving tended to be very general and nonspecific. Therefore, for the most part, it was unusable. Bill and his team not only helped us solve problems that had plagued us but also provided solutions to problems we had not realized existed.

Bill was an amazing man. He could tear a motor down to the stator and rotor and then find out what type of bearings were used and how well the motor was wound. Having Bill and Gulf Coast Fan and Light as our partners was like having an external engineering department that literally field-tested hundreds of thousands of ceiling fans. Thus, they provided us with not only the results of these tests but also the corrective measures to make a better fan. They pointed out and helped us solve a number of critical issues. Among these were noise-related issues such as clicking, humming, and wobbling. They also helped to improve the coupling systems and die-cast brackets. They worked with us to improve finishes and packaging as well. Out of the many inventions that King of Fans and I have created over the years, many were suggested by Bill and Gulf Coast Fan and Light. They taught us how the ceiling fans are installed and how to avoid problems that might arise in the field due to specific climate differences.

Bill and Gulf Coast Fan and Light were helpful to the entire ceiling fan industry. When we improved Old Jacksonville Ceiling Fans, everyone else in the industry seemed to follow. Bill helped to shape this industry toward higher quality, faster installation, and quiet, long-life reliability. He was passionate about fixing problems and making the best fan in the industry, and he was a credit to all who had the pleasure of knowing and working with him. May God bless Bill. I write this with love and my admiration.

* * *

By Jim Stewart

As one of Bill's best friends for many years, he asked that I write a foreword for his book.

My family and I have found Bill's poetry to be highly inspirational. The words have brought us closer to God and made us believe that the world would be a better place if we all just helped each other. At Bill's funeral, I was asked to speak about him, which was difficult considering how much I loved him as a friend. Knowing where he was going and not fearing death but accepting it with open arms, he was an inspiration to me. I believe after you read his poetry, you will feel the same way too.

Acknowledgements

We want to first acknowledge our God and his only born son, Jesus Christ, whom we believe has the power to save us from sin and without whom these poems would not have the power to help others. We want to acknowledge that he had everything to do with us finding each other in 1998 and marrying on November 13, 1999. He heard our heartfelt prayers to find the partner he had for each of us. We have been ardent companions and have experienced together the goodness of God. We are thankful for all of our family and for the blessings of parenting Olivia and Jay together for many years. We want to acknowledge our many mutual and individual friends who have crossed our paths and have made a difference in our lives for the better. We would like to thank our mothers, Genevieve and Ruth, for helping us grow up knowing we were loved and for nurturing good values in us. Our greatest hope is that you enjoy these writings and are blessed.

Bill and Terri Scheel

Section I:
Bill's Earlier Years

Try to Remember

Tonight is the night you have waited for.
The year is at its end.
So now you prepare to celebrate
And see the new one in.

There are so many wonderful places to go
And exciting sights to see.
You think of the good times you will have
And how good the next year will be.

Stop and take a moment, though,
To reflect on memories in your mind,
Memories of every shape and form
Of the year that is left behind.

It is lying lonely now,
Awaiting only death,
Saying farewell to all it's known
As it approaches its final breath.

Once it lived and flourished
And had its moments great.
Now it is lying motionless
As it faces its forefathers' fate.

You ask how a year lives and breathes
And feels as people do.
Don't you see this year you've lived
Is now a part of you?

It lived and breathed as you did.
It has been part of your life.
It may have brought you happiness,
Or love, or wealth, or strife.

It may have helped you find out who you are
Or just seemed to pass you by.
It may have dealt a crushing blow
Or helped you reach the sky.

Just realize this year, almost gone,
Is part of who you are,
And if you hadn't had its company,
You never would have come this far.

So, as you're waiting for its end,
Through the revelry and cheer,
Give a few silent moments of thought
For the end of a memorable year.

By William C. Scheel II in 1969 at the age of fifteen.

They Couldn't See

The war went on,
Went on for several years.
The war went on ignoring
All our human tears.

All the great warlords
Played their game of war,
While all the lesser people
Were forced to suffer more.

They all claimed they'd stop it.
None of them even tried.
All they did was stand there
While all of their soldiers died.

The war went on for several years.
The armies dwindled down,
Till each of the kingly warlords
Was stripped of his bloody crown.

They battled then, among themselves,
At least those left alive.
Look at all the lives they took,
But still they did survive.

But, in all their foolishness,
They managed to join the rest.
In all their blindness they couldn't see
No one can forcibly be the best.

To be the best or better,
You need love and an open heart.
But it seems all those people
Had been slaughtered from the start.

So, now, all you lords of war,
You rulers over men,
You had to fight as children
And cause the world to end.

By William C. Scheel II (1970s)

He's Not Really Gone

It seems too much to bear,
This loss of yours so great.
We know it's so unfair,
Be it accident or fate.

I've seen you go from loving warmth
To emptiness and despair.
I've tried everything I know
To show how much I care.

I didn't really know him long,
But I felt I had a friend.
I never dreamed a life so precious
Could come so quickly to an end.

He was a beautiful child indeed
With blond hair and eyes of blue.
His loving ways and friendliness
I'm sure he got from you.

Our world is not quite as bright
Now that your Randy's gone.
I know how hard it's been for you
To endure and carry on.

In this poem I'm sending you
All my love and prayers.
I want you and Ronnie to know
How much I really care.

I'm sure he is in heaven now,
Happy and at play.
And before he knows you're gone,
You'll be with him to stay.

So live life right and do the things
You know that you should do.
And when the time comes for you to go,
He'll spend an eternity with you.

By William C. Scheel II (1980)

This poem is dedicated to Babs and Ronnie Rucker. It was written for Babs and Ronnie when their four-year-old son drowned in New Braunfels in the Comal River at the Tube Chute.

True Friends

We all travel down the road of life,
Meeting friends along the way.
Some pass from our company quickly,
While others decide to stay.

Friends come in all shapes and sizes
From fat, to tall, to thin.
In reality, it's not the looks that count;
It's the person who lies within.

There are friends who like to party
And are always having fun.
And when the party's ended,
You will find that they are gone.

So, what happens when you hurt
And are laden with despair?
You feel you cannot go on
And the pain is too much to bear.

You reach out for your buddies
And find that you're alone.
It seems the party is over
And there is no one left at home.

That is when you discover true friends,
The ones who really care.
When all of your good-time buddies leave,
You will find your friends still there.

They take the time to listen;
They're concerned about how you feel.
It is in times of trouble when you find
Which friendships are truly real.

Never forget that having friends
Requires friendship too.
You need to care and be there
Just like they were with you.

So next time a friend is in trouble,
Stop and think before you walk away,
And never let yourself forget
That true friends are here to stay.

By William C. Scheel II (1980s)

Once Upon a Shelf

When it seems all is going wrong
And things are closing in.
When problems are all you seem to have,
And you're reaching your rope's end.

Take some time to realize
That you're sitting on a shelf.
It seems so very lonely there
With just your problems and yourself.

As you sit there, lost and alone,
You wonder what to do.
In all this time you've never noticed
All those people just like you.

Yes, they're surely out there,
Trying to survive.
Struggling through life from day to day
But never quite alive.

So, open up your eyes
And hop down off that shelf.
Find someone who needs a friend,
And you can help yourself.

A friendly smile, a helping hand,
A warm and open heart:
These are the things within yourself
That will help you make a start.

Start helping others with their problems,
And learn to share your own.
Before you know it, you'll be off that shelf,
And you'll know you're not alone.

This is just a simple recipe
To help you down life's road.
You'll find the world a much better place
When you learn to share the load.

By William C. Scheel II (1980s)

Mind and Heart

There are two things that guide us
Through our lives each day.
Both contribute to who we are
And work to guide our way.

Our minds are constantly analyzing
All the things we do.
They record all we see
And shape our point of view.

Our hearts bring us feelings
Of every shape and kind.
And for each record our minds have,
There is a feeling we can find.

Although they work hand in hand
Each and every day.
There are times that one says go
And the other tells us stay.

In these times of indecision
It's so hard to do what's right,
Because the two things we rely on
Just seem to want to fight.

Your heart says, "Do what you feel you need."
Your mind says, "No, that's wrong."
Your mind says, "Do what is right."
But your heart says, "The hurt's too strong."

Your mind tries to think clearly,
But it is drowning in despair.
Your heart has so many questions,
But your mind just isn't there.

Usually too late they find out
That all these things they do
Make things so much worse
For the place they live in you.

They try to trick each other
And try to ease the pain.
But every time they do,
It always seems in vain.

I don't know all the answers,
And sometimes I feel pain.
Sometimes I don't know what to do
And try too hard in vain.

I hope the people whom I love
Will try to really see
That some of these things I do
Are from the turmoil inside of me.

I believe there is a remedy
To this turmoil deep inside.
We have to turn and face it.
We cannot run and hide.

We have to be the very best
We know that we can be.
We have to believe in who we are
If we are ever to be free.

So, inside I am going to try
With every thing I do
To make both my mind and heart
To love and understand too.

By William C. Scheel II (1989)

      This poem was dedicated to Kimberly Dawn Stansell on March 21, 1989.

Sittin' On a Fence

Have you ever been on a fence
Just wondering what to do?
On one side lies your past,
On the other all that's new.

On the new side lies uncertainty
And things you just don't know.
The other feels so familiar,
The safer place to go.

The security of what you've known
Calls you back again once more.
It's so easy to forget why you left
The places you've been before.

Are you scared to take a step
Outside your comfort zone?
Is going back a guarantee
That you won't still be alone?

While you're still up on that fence,
Ask some questions from within.
Am I worth all I want
Or just what life has been?

Am I willing to compromise
My freedom and my friends?
And if so, can I keep giving in
To demand that never ends?

Do I have my freedom?
Am I all that I can be?
Is this past of mine
Not all, just part of me?

Am I really happy?
Do I feel complete?
Is security victory?
Or is compromise defeat?

Does my future hold a chance
To be all I can be?
To share who I really am,
To be happy and to be free?

Realize your future's yours.
The choice is yours to make.
Ask all you want from life.
It's there for you to take.

When you face the new side of things,
There will be risks to take.
But realize you're worth those risks.
It's your future that's at stake.

By William C. Scheel II (1990)

Football

To some football is just a game,
And as silly as it seems,
It captures so many imaginations
And fulfills so many dreams.

There are those who hate or ignore
This brutal game men play.
They just don't understand
Football fans on game day.

But if you look with open mind
Behind the football scenes,
There are more than just big kids
Who make up football teams.

There're young and old, rich and poor,
And men from every race.
There're those who coach and those who play
And those who just fill space.

But etched upon every face,
You'll find the threads that bind
Are heart and soul, blood and tears,
And a joining of their minds.

Conviction of commitment,
Courage, ability, and brains
Working toward a common goal
Through the triumphs and the pains.

To be your best when all seems lost
And never lose the flame.
To never waver from team goals
Through the disappointments and the fame.

It's not just learning how to win,
But how to lose with grace.
It's never giving up on yourself,
In even ultimate disgrace.

So, for those of you who don't understand
Why fans hold this game so dear,
Look at the excitement on their faces
During that special time of year.

The hopes and dreams of champions
Bring a magic to their life,
A chance to share a victory
Over the turmoil and the strife.

A common bond between strangers
Who suddenly are friends,
Riding this emotional rollercoaster
Until the very end.

And when the season is over,
And there are no more games to play,
The bond between football fans
Will never go away.

By William C. Scheel II (1991)

My Friend Kevin

Today I stand before you all
Wondering what to say.
Questioning why my best friend had to die
in such a cruel and tragic way.

I remember the first day we met.
It seems so long ago.
We were both so young and crazy
With so much yet to know.

There is no doubt he was blessed
With the gift to square dance call.
And he traveled around the country,
Calling dances big and small.

But even more a gift
Was his ability to teach.
He made every student feel
Success within their reach.

He made so many people happy
As he traveled far and wide.
But not too many people knew
The Kevin deep inside.

I had known him better than anyone,
At least that's how it seems.
We shared so many secrets
about our hopes and our dreams.

He gave himself to the people he loved
For the majority of his life.
But there was always something missing.
He longed for children and a wife.

But through all the years I knew him,
He gave his heart to only one.
And Cyndi, his wife, and his daughters
Became his stars, his moon, and sun.

I found I really missed him
As we parted on life's road.
But I knew he'd always be there
To help me share life's load.

And now I'm here before you.
Is he finally gone to stay?
Or has God called him
And helped to light his way.

I do know he was happier
Than he'd ever been before.
His dreams and prayers were answered.
He had discovered so much more.

He had searched so very long and hard
Before his dreams came true.
I'm here to say, "Cyndi, Amber, and Robyn,
He gave his life to you."

I feel the emptiness in our hearts
As we struggle with good-bye.
What answer could there be
To the haunting question, "Why?"

I think he would want his memories
To put a smile upon my face.
He would want us to be happy
And make the world a better place.

And though we can't touch or see him,
He is here with us today.
And through our thoughts and memories,
He will never fade away.

By William C. Scheel II

This poem was dedicated to Cyndi, Amber, and Robyn Bacon on December 30, 1993. It was written in memory of my friend Kevin R. Bacon (October 12, 1956 to December 27, 1993). On December 27, 1993, Kevin, his wife, and his two children were having a meal in the food court of the Irving Mall when a fight erupted between two rival gangs. One of the gang members pulled a gun and started shooting. A stray bullet caught Kevin in the head. He died instantly.

My Dearest Hungee

My Dearest Hungee,

You are the apple of my eye, the leaves on my tree, the other half of my soul, and a part of me.

In Christ we met, and in Christ we love; we have found true freedom through the word from above.

I thank Jesus every day of my life for the blessing he gave me in you, my wife.

When fear comes to try to deceive, we weather the storm, for to Jesus we cleave.

Through pain and strife or good times and fun, we know we're complete because in Jesus we're one!

All my love, always.

Your Hungee,
Bill

By William C. Scheel II

This poem was written for my lovely bride in early 2000.

Section II: Bill's Later Years

Family

A Mom's Undying Love

Moms are a gift from the Lord,
Given to each and every one.
The love and care they give a child
Is God's work being done.

The miracle of the mother's womb
Is a testament to God's glory.
From there came God's many gifts
In story after story.

Through the womb of Sarah,
God brought forth his nation.
And through the Virgin Mary,
He gave us Jesus, Lord of Creation.

The experience of childbirth
Is like no other that we know.
For months inside her womb,
A mother feels her baby grow.

The pain that she endures
During her baby's birth
Forms a bond between them
That's immeasurable in its worth.

God's calling for new mothers
Is her baby's love and care.
Through her love and nurturing,
God's presence is always there.

As her baby starts to grow
Right before her eyes,
She is there to teach and love
And comfort when it cries.

They seem to grow up so fast,
The first word, and then they're talking.
Next comes that first step they take.
And soon after, they are walking.

Now they are into everything,
Running here and there.
They start asking all those questions,
And God's wisdom is your prayer.

You give them God's correction
And discipline as you must.
The value of God's wisdom
Will increase their love and trust.

Next it's time to go to school
For the first time on their own.
You pray that they'll be safe
And feel welcome, not alone.

You do your best to teach them
And raise them in God's ways.
You pray that all your efforts
Will last them all their days.

The older they get, the more they learn
About life and reality.
Their opinions and their beliefs
Develop their personality.

First friendships and adventure,
Then they want to start dating.
Things are moving so fast,
You have a hard time relating.

Now it's time for them to drive,
It's more control you're losing.
You pray that when decisions come
It's God's wisdom they're choosing.

Then the independence comes,
And now they know it all.
How did all of your wisdom
So quickly take a fall?

As life's lessons educate,
They start to understand.
Now you are smart again,
And they're ready for a hand.

As they grow and fall in love,
They say it's time to marry.
Now the thought of losing them
Is really very scary.

When they are on their own
You pray they have God's wisdom.
All you can do is love them now
And trust that God is with them.

For the rest of your life to you
Your child will always be,
The child you held and nurtured
And bounced upon your knee.

I am thankful everyday
For the gift from God above.
That special gift from heaven
Of a mom's undying love.

By William C. Scheel II

   This poem is dedicated to: Genevieve J. Scheel, my "MomO" (February 14, 1918, to September 3, 2009).

Blessed Be the Dad

Our Father, Mighty God,
Is the lord of all creation.
He created man and woman
And a means for their salvation.

As woman came from man,
So God assigned authority.
The dad, then the mom
Is the order of God's priority.

The dad is the one
Whom God holds accountable.
When the dad trusts in God,
No challenge is insurmountable.

When sin takes the dad,
God's plan is interrupted.
The enemy swoops in,
And soon all are corrupted.

God calls the dad
To cherish his lovely bride
And for better or for worse
To remain steadfastly by her side.

He is to be the provider
Of all his family's needs.
He is to minister God's word
Through his speech and through his deeds.

He is to guide his children.
In the ways of the Lord.
And through God's discipline,
Their obedience will be restored.

He is to be the protector
From physical and spiritual harm.
He is to call on Mighty God
To defend and to disarm.

He is called to be faithful
And loving to his wife.
He is to make God and his family
The priorities of his life.

When the dad's an obedient servant
And walks in God's ways,
Blessed be the dad
Who is worthy of God's praise.

By William C. Scheel II

Marriage Is God's Miracle

The miracle of marriage
Is God's enduring love.
And as we become one flesh,
It's God's kingdom we're part of.

Marriage can be God's miracle,
Though not in every case.
It can be everlasting love
Or end in heartache and disgrace.

When God set forth his plan
To unite a man and wife,
His Holy vows defined that
It should be for life.

We are to have and to hold each other
Just like a precious jewel.
God shows us how to do this
With his Golden Rule.

For better or for worse
Is joy or suffering without measure.
God's peace will fill our lives
When his word is our treasure.

For richer or for poorer
Defines our earthly state.
But the riches of God's love
Is what makes a marriage great.

In sickness and in health
Describes our physical condition.
No matter what we go through,
God's love should be our mission.

To love and to cherish
Each other as we are one.
To sacrifice for each other
As God did his only son.

How long should this go on?
Till death do us part,
Together, enduring all,
With God's love in our shared heart.

If your marriage feels empty
And you've decided to look around,
Have you become complacent
About the love that you found?

Don't settle for divorce.
Cast down the devil's lies.
When you turn your heart to God,
He will always hear your cries.

No matter how bad things are,
The miracle of marriage is still there.
When God's love fills your heart,
There's nothing God can't repair.

It begins with God's forgiveness
For yourself and for your spouse.
Invite Jesus into your lives
And bring God's word into your house.

Remember the love you had
Before you drifted apart.
Find that special person you met.
It's never too late to start.

From this very day forward,
Speak your holy vows again.
Pledge your faithfulness to God.
The victory is yours to win.

As you let go of guilt and fear
And commit yourselves to one another,
God's miracle of marriage
Will be the blessing you discover.

By William C. Scheel II

1 Corinthians 13:4-7. Love is patient, love is kind. It does not envy, it does not boast, it is not proud. It does not dishonor others, it is not self-seeking, it is not easily angered, it keeps no record of wrongs. Love does not delight in evil but rejoices with the truth. It always protects, always trusts, always hopes, always perseveres.

Colossians 3:18-21 Wives, submit yourselves unto your husbands, as it is fitting the Lord. Husbands, love your wives and do not be harsh them. Children, obey your parents in all things, for this pleases the Lord. Fathers, do not embitter your children, or they will become discouraged.

Soul Searching

Any Minute

Time marches on.
We're just along for the ride.
The length of our trip
Is for God to decide.

It's not how long we're aboard
This planet called Earth;
It's how we use our time here
That determines our worth.

God has a plan
For each of our lives.
The choices we make
Will be our success or demise.

What is your focus?
How do you live?
Do you love or do you hate?
Do you take or do you give?

Is your life ruled
By ambition and sin?
Has selfishness created
The mess that you're in?

Do you wander through life
With no aim or direction?
Do you rebel
When it's time for correction?

Have you lived your life
To serve the Lord?
Are heaven's promises
To be your reward?

What if today,
Most of your time disappeared
And your years turned to days,
Have you persevered?

What would the things
You value and do
Say to the world
And reveal about you?

Would your priorities change
In your time that remained?
Would you search for more
Than just to be entertained?

Would the thought of death
Being so near
All of a sudden
Create doubt and fear?

Where will I be
When my life comes to an end?
Will there be time
To repent and amend?

Is heaven or hell
To be my fate?
I pray, O God,
That it's not too late.

Focus on God's work,
Claim Jesus as savior,
And change your life
Through your heart and behavior.

There's only one price
For the debt of your sin.
Alone, you lose;
With Jesus, you win.

Alone before God,
Your debt of sin is eternal.
The place you will go
Will be infernal.

With Jesus there,
Your sin will be covered.
Eternity with God
Will be your future discovered.

If all of these questions
Have caused you to think,
Realize every moment
We stand on the brink.

What if your life stopped
Without time for reflection?
Where would you go
When you faced God's inspection?

You can change your life.
Invite Jesus in it.
Your last stop on earth
Could be any minute.

By William C. Scheel II

Broken Ground

Broken ground is a place
Where all of us have been.
Darkness surrounds us, and it seems
Our world is caving in.

When life is good and we are safe,
We don't need assistance.
Our good fortune and well-being
Will carry us the distance.

I'm so smart, I can't fail.
I studied really hard.
I'm talented beyond compare.
There's much in which I've starred.

Behold the empire that I built.
Now I am surely in control.
Hey, I just won the lotto.
Look at me; I'm on a roll.

The desires of your heart
Define your scale of measure.
Is your happiness and success
Based on worldly treasure?

When trouble strikes you hard and fast,
How are you affected?
You never had a use for God,
But now you want to be connected.

The magnitude of each ordeal
Is based upon your perception.
As fear creeps in, do you succumb
To the devil's deception?

Know that God is always there
As you live life day to day.
But were you so busy in your life,
He just got in your way?

So busy doing this and that,
It's not what you'd call sin.
But now that tragedy has struck,
You want to let God in.

You may have sat in church for years.
You saw him every Sunday.
But where was he in your life
When it came to Monday?

What's the difference between
The casual Christian and the sinner?
One thinks he knows the Lord,
And one's a worldly winner.

As our world of security's challenged,
Like it was on 9/11,
We realize we're not in control,
And we raise our hands to heaven.

Our life becomes broken ground
Into which our security is falling.
This is the time and the place;
We are ready to hear God's calling.

God gave the gift of forgiveness
Through the death of his son, Jesus.
He allowed the death of his only son
In order that he could free us.

All he asks us in return
Is to die in our sinful ways.
We are to become a new self in Jesus
And be faithful all our days.

God doesn't promise us painless lives.
We suffer for his glory.
It's when we are weak that he is great
And God's victory is our story.

Are you are in a place
Where your future is in doubt,
When you have looked everywhere
And there's no one to help you out?

The time has come to seek out God
And ask for his forgiveness.
Invite Jesus into your heart,
And become a Christian witness.

When Jesus becomes your shinning light,
Those earthly things won't matter.
The veil of darkness will be lifted,
And worldly demons all will scatter.

A peace will come into your life,
And a joy will fill your heart.
So, surrender yourself to the Lord.
Right now's the time to start.

Just speak these words out loud,
"Jesus you are my lord and savior.
In you I am born again.
I will change my heart and my behavior."

Make him lord of your life,
And devalue earthly pleasure.
When you put him first in your heart,
You build up heavenly treasure.

Spread the news, share his word,
And through his words you've spoken.
The lost and lonely can be reached
When their ground is finally broken.

By William C. Scheel II

Don't Be the Devil's Toy

We are all children of the world
When our life begins.
The path we take along the way
Determines how life ends.

There will be good times and bad,
Of that there is no doubt.
How we handle the highs and lows
Is for us to figure out.

We all want to be happy.
The true question is how.
We look for things in our life
To make us happy now.

Suffering is not an option;
It takes our happiness away.
Our mind searches for the things
That will bring us happiness today.

But where do we search for happiness?
We think it's everywhere.
If I could just have what they have,
I wouldn't have a care.

If I just had that special person,
I'm sure that would be enough.
If I were popular and good looking,
Life wouldn't be so tough.

What if I was famous?
I'd be happy then.
If I could just win the lotto,
All my problems soon would end.

I know that special drug
Will make despair disappear.
If I can get another drink,
Then I will have no fear.

Happiness is fleeting
And can be very hard to find.
The reason is our emotions
Are a changing state of mind.

When our minds rule our lives,
It's limited to what we know.
And when our life is trouble filled,
We don't know where to go.

Our happiness has failed us.
We feel lost and confused.
We've lived our lives the best we can,
And all we feel is abused.

In these times, we can't give up.
Life doesn't just go away.
We need to seek out God
If we want the dawn of a new day.

God is always waiting
To catch us when we fall.
He sent us his son, Jesus,
To show his love for all.

The good news is through Jesus
We always have a friend.
And even in our darkest hours,
He'll be with us till the end.

Happiness may come and go,
As all our feelings do.
The Lord can bring peace to your heart,
No matter what you struggle through.

When you give your heart to God,
He fills it up with love.
Joy is this inner peace
That comes from God above.

Joy comes from letting go
Of all the things we fear.
Even though life has its trials,
Peace fills us when God is near.

The truth is God loves us all so much.
He has an eternal plan.
He sent his son to the earth
To live life as a man.

Jesus's life is an example
Of how we all should live.
He teaches us to be filled with love,
And Joy comes when we give.

Even though he was innocent,
He died to save our souls.
He teaches us to overcome the world
And gives us all new goals.

Through him we are born again,
And from sin we are set free.
He wants us all to walk his walk,
And he will give us new eyes to see.

Is happiness too hard to find
And you just aren't satisfied?
Do you have an empty feeling
No matter what you've tried?

Jesus is the answer.
Trade your happiness for joy.
Embrace his love and peace,
And don't be the devil's toy.

By William C. Scheel II

Inside Out

Everywhere we look today,
The superficial thrives.
How do the way things look and sound
Truly affect our lives?

The flashy politician
Who knows just what to say.
The criminal sports hero
Who was acquitted yesterday.

Bulimic supermodels
Who look so thin and gaunt.
Power-wielding billionaires
Who can have anything they want.

Famous movie stars
Who give their face another lift.
Popular sex symbols
With personal lives adrift.

This list of worldly heroes
Goes on and never quits.
They have the best the world can offer,
Yet their lives still give them fits.

With popularity as wide as the ocean
And character deep as a puddle,
Their search for true happiness
Continues to confound and befuddle.

When fame and worldly treasure
Become your lifelong goal,
Is the bounty of your gain
Really worth your soul?

Are all these worldly heroes
What life is all about?
How attractive would they look
If you could turn them inside out?

Do you know the story
Of a man named Dorian Gray?
He decided to sell his soul,
So forever young he'd stay.

His portrait is what would age
While he retained his youth.
As he filled his life with sin,
Only his portrait revealed the truth.

Finally, in a rage,
He stabbed the portrait with a knife,
But the knife entered his heart, and
His horrid corpse revealed his life.

Ask yourself a question,
Are you like Dorian Gray?
He was willing to sell his soul
For what he could have today.

Is your success in this world
The scale you use to measure?
The Lord, God Almighty says,
"Don't store up earthly treasure."

God tells us to clothe ourselves
With compassion, kindness, and humility.
The true worth of our lives
Isn't ours, but his ability.

For God so loved the world
That he gave his only son.
When Jesus died and rose again,
God's defeat of death was done.

When we keep Jesus in our hearts
And his love's what we're about.
We will show the world his love
When we wear our insides out.

By William C. Scheel II

Right Now

We all are faced with the choice
Whether to do right or wrong.
We all have times in our lives
When we're weak or strong.

We can reflect upon our past
And see the errors of our ways.
We can plan to do what's right
For the remainder of our days.

God gave us free will.
It's up to us to choose.
Will the path that we take
Cause us to win or to lose?

When we ignore God's wisdom
On the path that we travel,
The wickedness of the world
Can cause our lives to unravel.

In the moments that we suffer
For the choices that we made,
We remember our wrong decisions
And the reasons that we strayed.

We make a promise to ourselves
To change our evil ways.
We turn our eyes toward God
And make promises to praise.

"God, if only you will help me,
I will change the things I do.
Just rescue me from my peril.
I know I can count on you."

But as soon as we are safe,
Our promises seem to fade.
We go back to where we were,
Secure and unafraid.

There's only one true way to change
The path of life's direction.
We must devote ourselves to God
And embrace God's correction.

It's easy to commit to change.
We will even give a date.
"O Lord, I'll start tomorrow.
I'm sure it's not too late."

There's a problem with that thinking.
Tomorrow never arrives.
If we don't change today,
We will never change our lives.

Embrace God's mighty wisdom.
Say no to evil things.
Claim Jesus as your savior.
Embrace the forgiveness that he brings.

There is only one time we have
To decide what we won't allow.
It's not tomorrow or yesterday.
We have to start right now.

By William C. Scheel II

Sin Is a Monkey Trap

From the very beginning,
When Eve ate the apple,
Sin became the struggle
With which we all must grapple.

Now we are estranged from God,
Through this trap called sin.
God devised a plan
To correct this mess we're in.

When God spoke to the serpent,
His plan he did reveal.
"He will crush your head,
And you will strike his heel."

The Word of God tells us
That "he" is God's son, Jesus.
God sent his son to die,
So his innocent death could free us.

Satan tried and tried
To defeat God's perfect plan.
He struck at Jesus's heel
To retain his victory over man.

But Jesus, in perfect wisdom,
Never went astray.
He crushed Satan's head
On his resurrection day.

Even after defeat,
Sin is still Satan's power.
When we become sin's slave,
We'll be Satan's to devour.

A monkey trap's unique.
It's a container filled with bait.
It has only a small opening for access.
The monkey's choice becomes his fate.

When the monkey grabs the bait.
His hand becomes enlarged.
And unless he let's go,
He will never be discharged.

Just like a monkey trap,
Sin is Satan's trick.
We can hold on or let go.
It's up to us to pick.

God gave us victory in Jesus.
The choice is ours to make.
Do we hold onto our sin
And give victory to the snake?

Or do we let go of the sin
That will surely bring destruction?
As we make Jesus our lord and savior,
We will turn from sin's seduction.

You need to read God's word
And put it in your heart.
As we emulate Christ Jesus,
We become God's works of art.

So if you're feeling empty,
Let Jesus fill the gap.
He's the only one who can free us
From Satan's monkey trap.

By William C. Scheel II

Proverbs 11:6. The righteousness of the upright delivers them, but the unfaithful are trapped by evil desires.

Then What?

One day I was asked a question:
What is your life plan?
Is the course of your life
To be ruled by God or by man?

I know that there's a God,
And I've heard about his son.
But all of that religious stuff
Doesn't sound like fun.

Why are you asking me this question?
You're rushing things it seems.
I'm sure that in time I'll realize
All my hopes and dreams.

I guess a career will be my focus,
And success will be my goal.
I will educate myself
And prepare for my new role.

Then What?

I will search out my career
And prepare to move ahead.
Then I'll find a mate,
And we will both be wed.

Then What?

Where you're going with this question
Truly has me perplexed.
Isn't the answer obvious?
Of course our kids are next.

Then What?

I will work so very hard,
So I can provide the most life brings.
I want to raise my kids
And give my family the best of things.

Then What?

I will put my kids through college
And I'll be the best at what I do.
Our worth will be defined
By all that we accrue.

Then What?

My kids will be successful,
And I will retire with my wealth.
I will exercise and eat right,
So I will have good health.

Then What?

I will be a great grandparent
And focus on family unity.
I will do charitable things
And be a pillar of the community.

Then What?

The only thing that's left, I guess;
It'll be time for me to die.
I know I've lived a good life
And have favor with God on high.

Then What?

I will stand before Mighty God
And show him all I've done.
So what will be your answer
When God asks about his son?

I went to church all those years.
I said that God is king.
I claimed Jesus as my savior,
But I guess I didn't change a thing.

Then, Mighty God's answer
Caught me by surprise.
"You never really knew my son
Through your life of compromise "

"I'm sorry to say, my son,
You're name just isn't here."
Then, all of a sudden, my heart
Was filled with doubt and fear.

Hey, get your hands off of me!
God, they're taking me away!
"Yes, my son, they are.
It's your final judgment day."

I woke up in a cold sweat
And fell to bended knee.
O Jesus, you are my savior!
O God, please hear my plea!

I know what I must do
To avoid this awful fate.
I must live my life for Jesus.
I'm blessed it's not too late.

So, if you die tomorrow,
And you stand before the Lord,
For the life you've chosen to live
What will be your just reward?

I thank God I had that nightmare
Filled with fear and pain.
And even still today that question
Keeps echoing in my brain.

Then what?

By William C. Scheel II

Your Life and the Titanic

Your life and the Titanic
Are partners in their fate.
One's end is still unknown;
The other's, we know the date.

You were made by God.
The Titanic was made by man.
The Titanic has met its end,
But for you, God has a plan.

They boasted about Titanic,
That it was ridiculous to think
That even Mighty God
Could cause this ship to sink.

Sailing smoothly and peacefully,
All were secure without a care.
No one knew beforehand
Of the iceberg waiting there.

The night was so dark and the water so calm,
It looked just like a mirror.
But with no waves to sound alarm,
They unknowingly drew nearer.

When they finally saw the iceberg,
They had no time to think.
They tried everything to miss it,
But as it struck, she began to sink.

The captain ignored several warnings
Through either overconfidence or distraction.
It was his total lack of wisdom
That led to the deadly chain reaction.

Are you listening for God's warnings?
Or are they easy to ignore?
Do you have a plan for your salvation
Before you reach death's door?

Pride goes before destruction,
a haughty spirit before a fall.
You may be sailing on smooth waters,
But you're headed for a squall,

Just like the builders of Titanic,
You dismiss God's mighty power.
Filled with arrogance and pride,
You will be the devil's to devour.

Or maybe your religion
Will be your saving grace.
You sit in church every Sunday,
But do you ever see God's face?

It's easy to hear God's word
And believe what is convenient.
You know God wants you to prosper,
And his judgment is surely lenient.

No matter whether you shun God's word
Or in his word you are selective,
Disaster is waiting up ahead
When you ignore God's directive.

Is your iceberg up ahead?
Can you survive the collision?
Will you be drowning in panic,
Or be saved by God's provision?

No one who denies the Son has the Father,
Is what God's word plainly states.
Without Jesus as your lifeboat,
An eternity without God awaits.

God has sent his lifeboat
To save us from destruction.
Through Jesus we are saved,
So look to God's word for instruction.

The Titanic is now gone,
But your life is still afloat.
Will your end take you by surprise,
Or will you be in God's lifeboat?

When God's word controls your life,
There's no need to panic.
With Jesus as your lifeboat,
You will be a survivor of life's Titanic.

By William C. Scheel II, inspired by Adrian Rogers.

Stuff

Without it, life is tough.

Stuff

I can never get enough.

Stuff

I really love to shop.

Stuff

I wish that I could stop!

Stuff

I need another sale.

Stuff

My stuff has me in jail.

Stuff

It's comin' out my ears.

Stuff

I've been collecting it for years.

Stuff

It takes up all my time.

Stuff

I haven't got a dime.

Stuff

It has to go away.

Stuff

God, please take it all away!

By William C. Scheel II

Belief is Relief

It seems there's no relief today
From the pressures that life brings
There is so much we have to deal with
When we fill our life with things.

There's pressure all around us
To get the latest stuff.
The true problem is
That we can never get enough.

The faster car, the nicer home,
That new diamond ring for your wife.
Only the best schools for your kids,
You want the finer things in life.

Surely as success grows
And begins to take effect,
The things that are truly important
Become the things that we neglect.

Some go to church on Sunday
To listen to God's word,
But we are so consumed with life,
His message mostly goes unheard.

Others of us consider Sunday
To be our recreation day.
There is so much for us to do.
It's our only day away.

Dad's out on the golf course.
Mom's hanging with her friends.
The kids are at the mall,
And the separation never ends.

As our separation grows
The enemy lies in wait.
And if we aren't aware,
It can be too late.

Mom has a drinking problem,
And dad is never home.
The kids are doing drugs,
And everyone's alone.

It all starts to consume us.
The pressure grows and grows.
And as life closes in,
We hope that nobody knows.

As we bury our ugly secrets,
It leaves us alone and feeling lost.
And the longer this continues,
The greater becomes the cost.

When you are alone in the darkness
And hopelessness begins to take its toll,
You can feel as though you're in a battle
For the possession of your soul.

Who you need is a friend,
Someone who you can trust.
He will hear your heart not judging,
Never revealing what you've discussed.

He is the one who always stand beside you
Through trial and tribulation.
He is one who you can always rely on
In every situation.

The great news: there is a friend.
He is there for us all,
Waiting with open arms.
All you have to do is call.

I am sure that you know his name.
He's Jesus, God's only son.
His life is a perfect example
Of God's work being done.

You may only know his name
Or not believe in him at all.
The truth is he patiently waiting
Just to hear your call.

As you call on Jesus
And confess your sinful ways,
A joy and peace will fill you
That truly does amaze.

You need to examine every priority
That has given your life direction.
Make him the priority of your life,
And submit to his correction.

His joy will fill your heart,
And he will heal you from your grief.
As you believe in his awesome power,
You'll discover belief is relief.

By William C. Scheel II

Godly Values

My Prayer

My Prayer is that whether
My time left is short or long,
That I will see it through,
And I will finish strong.

No matter what I face,
I will have no fear.
Peace fills my heart,
For Jesus is always near.

By William C. Scheel II

The Power of the Tongue

Other's words impact our lives,
Whether for better or for worse.
The way we choose to use our tongue
Can be a blessing or a curse.

Think of a rudder on a ship.
It determines the ship's direction.
The fate of those aboard
Rests on the captain's course selection.

Do you ever think about your tongue?
It's really not that large.
But the power that it wields, good or bad,
Depends on who's in charge.

The tongue that brings healing is a tree of life,
But a deceitful tongue crushes the spirit.
It reveals the content of our heart,
And affects all who hear it.

A great deal of pain we have
Comes from what's been said.
Words can cut like a knife
And echo in your head.

When we're consumed with anger
And don't care what we say,
The pain that we deliver
May never go away.

A wise man's heart guides his mouth
And his lips promote instruction.
When God's word is our council,
God's love is our conduction.

We need to think before we speak
Each and every day.
Soon the words we love to hear
Will become the words we say.

When we cast down words that curse
And use God's word to heal,
The true power of the tongue
Is the blessing that we reveal.

By William C. Scheel

To Forgive is to Forget

I want you to stop and think
Of all the baggage that you carry.
Is the hurt and bitterness you have
Really kind of scary?

You don't think about it all at once,
Just from time to time.
A person here and a person there
That you'll punish for each crime.

How someone stole from you
Or proceeded to wreck your life.
How they stabbed you in the back
Or took your husband or your wife.

The list just goes on and on
In a countless number of ways.
And the pain we carry in our mind
Can follow us all our days.

Those hurtful memories
In our minds are crystal clear.
They can shape the paths of our lives
And can fill us all with fear.

The fear of being hurt
Or of being lost and alone.
The pain of humiliation
Or of losing all we own.

Ask yourself this question:
Does this bitterness I hold
Bring peace into my life
Or leave me feeling very cold?

As the pain in us grows,
It's harder to keep concealed.
And through our outward actions,
Our true character is revealed.

We've said words of forgiveness.
They weren't that hard to say.
But the memories of their offenses
Are as clear as yesterday.

We told them that we'd let it go
(As long as they behave).
But when they stepped out of line,
We forgot that we forgave.

And then there are those times
When forgiveness is not an option.
What they did to injure us
Can never be forgotten.

As time goes on, it all adds up.
The baggage grows and grows.
It pushes out our love and peace
Until it overflows.

No matter how much we think
We repay others for their sin,
The only thing that it does
Is define the prison that we're in.

When we are the transgressors,
It's forgiveness we expect,
But when the shoe's on the other foot,
It's easy to reject.

We all have something in common:
We are sinners before the Lord.
And the debt that we owe to God,
None of us can afford.

God knows all we've done
And every sin that we commit.
Do you want to be accountable
Or do you want him to forget?

God made a way to forgive our sin
When Jesus died for all.
We are the sinners here,
But Jesus took the fall.

There are those who don't know him yet
And those who never will.
There are those who call his name
And trust he paid our bill.

If you don't know Jesus yet,
He can set you free.
He forgives all our sins,
And he died for you and me.

For all of you who call his name
To wash away your sin,
Be very careful about
Your bitterness within.

God gave us all the key
To what we all must do.
You must forgive everyone
Who has done something to you.

God gave us a reminder.
We all know the prayer.
The only way to be forgiven
Is waiting for us there.

Forgive us our trespasses
As we forgive those who trespass against us.
If we can't forgive,
It's not in Jesus that we trust.

How can we be forgiven
In Jesus's precious name
When we continue to harden our hearts
And pass out hurt and blame?

You need to have a meeting
With that person over your sink.
You need to let all your baggage go
And change the way you think.

God tells us through his son,
You can lay your sin to rest,
But only when you forgive
And get things off of your chest.

You have to wipe your memory clean,
As Jesus has done for you.
Fill the void with joy and love,
And you can start anew.

There is a way to discuss the hurt
With those who cause us pain.
We need to do it all in love,
And we can wipe away the stain.

There is no transgression so great
That through Christ we can't forget.
He calls us all to forgive
And cancel every debt.

And when we stand before the Lord
On our final judgment day,
Jesus forgives by forgetting our sin,
And our past is washed away.

By William C. Scheel II

Trust in the Truth

Trust is a valued trait.
It's something we must earn
To trust casts out fear
And is difficult to learn.

It's true trust has its risks,
But without it we are lost.
Fear becomes a way of life
And our peace becomes the cost.

Trust can be a treasure
In the peace that it brings.
It can also be a curse
When we trust in the wrong things.

When in God's holy word
We truly place our trust,
We are standing on the rock,
For he is righteous and is just.

But when we trust in the world
And selfish motives are our goal,
We let down our defenses
And the enemy takes control.

In trust there is a peace
That we will achieve.
Peace and love are ours
When in God's son we believe.

"Do not let your hearts be troubled.
Trust in God, trust also in me,"
Jesus tells us with these words
The way that God set us free.

Free from doubt and fear
And the loneliness that it brings.
Free from the enemy's clutches
As we cast down selfish things.

"I am, the way, the truth, and the life,"
Jesus did proclaim.
"I am the only way to the Father."
We can trust in Jesus's name.

As we trust in him,
We are filled with love and joy.
As we share his precious love,
The enemy's kingdom we'll destroy.

If you're feeling lost and lonely,
And life's set you adrift.
If fear and doubt have gripped you,
And you really need a lift.

It doesn't matter if you're old
Or in the prime of youth,
God's kingdom can be yours
When you trust in the truth.

By William C. Scheel II

Your Shadow

The Lord our God is the author of light,
Which shines down from above on us all.
When he is the high point of our life,
There is no place for darkness to fall.

But as we become distracted by other things
And God is not quite as high in our sky,
We will see a shadow begin to appear,
A place of darkness where the enemy will lie.

The further we stray from God's precious light,
The larger our shadow will grow.
The darkness expands and the enemy waits
To deliver his death-yielding blow.

To keep God's light high in our sky
Is to keep his precious word always near.
His love and forgiveness will comfort us all
And remove all of our doubt and fear.

Grow in God's word and accept Jesus as lord.
Live like he did everyday.
He is The Way and The Truth and The Life.
We are blessed when in his presence we stay.

As sinners, we must always be on guard
Not to heed the world's sinful call.
If you see your shadow begin to appear,
God's word can steer you from a fall.

When Jesus becomes the light of your life
And your walk becomes to love and to give,
The light that surrounds you will eliminate
A place for the darkness to live.

By William C. Scheel II

A Servant's Heart

Servant's Heart

Everywhere we look today
The philosophy that dwells
Defines our life's success
By what we attain for ourselves.

We are told we can find happiness
By being the best that we can be.
Self-help and self-indulgence
Are the world's reality.

When happiness and wealth
Are how you define success,
Where do you turn when life
Takes all that you possess?

When things are going smoothly
It's easy for us to be our master,
But we wonder why we're alone
When we face disaster.

As life takes a turn
And we're no longer in control,
The loneliness and fear
Can really take a toll.

God has a different plan
For each and every one.
God's model for our life
Is Jesus, God's only son.

Jesus's life teaches us
To always seek God's will.
He took the world's sin upon himself,
And through his death, he paid our bill.

What if Jesus had made himself
His first and highest priority?
Our sins would be ours to bear
If he had turned from God's authority.

But through his shining example
Of his selfless attitude,
He filled the lives that he blessed
With an eternal gratitude.

Jesus told us all,
"For he who is least among you shall be great."
But being least is an idea
To which the world just can't relate.

But when our goals become his
And serving others becomes our mission,
The path to peace and happiness
Will be our ultimate transition.

When we become God's tools
And we get out of God's way.
It allows his glory to shine through us
All he asks is that we obey.

When we live for Jesus
And obey God's holy word.
By giving selfless love and sacrifice,
Through us, God's voice is heard.

We no longer are lost and alone;
God's presence is always there.
And our lives will be rewarded
By his blessings that we share.

For as we give to others,
It's through others that we receive.
It's really not that hard;
All we have to do is believe.

When in God's eternal plan
Is what we choose to invest,
Our selfless love and giving
Is God's definition of success.

In the world you will never find
True peace and serenity
When all you focus on
Is your own divinity.

To reach God's eternal kingdom,
We must embrace God's holy son.
We must live for others first
And make him number one.

Cast worldly values down.
It's time for a new start.
Eternal blessings can be yours
When you have a servant's heart.

By William C. Scheel II

The Craftsman

We all start out on equal ground
At the moment of our birth.
The knowledge gained as we grow
Will be the measure of our worth.

Knowledge is the information
That we process everyday.
It is an ongoing fact of life
Whether at peace or in the fray.

Knowledge, as we live our lives
Is impossible to avoid.
It fills our minds; it affects our lives.
It makes us happy or annoyed.

I see knowledge like a tool
There for each of us to use.
Some use it constructively,
While others use it to abuse.

Like any tool created,
It needs a craftsman's touch.
The finest tool in untrained hands
Won't deliver near as much.

Wisdom is that craftsman's hand
That guides our knowledge true.
And as life's pitfalls come and go,
It works to guide us through.

The tool of knowledge is limitless.
It's up to us to fill our box.
Have we stored up quality
Or just filled it with rocks?

In every situation faced,
We must choose a knowledge tool.
The choice made can bring success
Or leave us feeling like a fool.

Have you ever been in a situation
Where knowledge led you astray?
You grabbed a rock from your box
And proceeded to bash away.

You may not even have known
Which tool was in your hand.
You caused hurt to so many,
And you still don't understand.

How can we gain the wisdom
For the use of every tool?
Just like every craftsman,
We have to go to school.

There is a source for wisdom
That we all can afford.
All we have to do is seek it.
It comes straight from the Lord.

When we let the Lord be our teacher,
He will show us the way.
He can give us a craftsman's hand
And wisdom everyday.

A great place to start
Is to learn the Golden Rule.
Do unto others as you would have
Them do unto you.

Be honorable and upright.
Be a source of joy and love.
Speak only what is true
And have faith in God above.

Bring peace into your heart
And put that fear away.
Be selfless in your actions.
You can start today.

God gave the greatest gift
That you can ever give.
He gave the life of his son,
So that all of us can live.

But for that gift to bless us,
Jesus had to make the choice:
To walk away and save his life
Or to obey his father's voice.

He chose to die a horrible death
To wash away our sin.
His earthly life he had to lose
For all of us to win.

He asks us to die to sin
So that we can be set free.
We can leave the bondage of the world
And live for eternity.

We need to talk and walk with him
And make him our best friend.
When you keep him in your life,
You will be a winner in the end.

You will acquire the knowledge
To work in other people's lives.
Knowledge with Godly wisdom
Produces fruit in God that thrives.

As you grow you will become
A craftsman for the Son.
And with Jesus by your side,
You can count the battle won.

By William C. Scheel II

The Faithful Farmer

There once was a farmer
Who so loved the Lord
That he prayed and he prayed
For his just reward.

First week after week,
Then year after year,
He patiently watched
For his crops to appear.

He sang praises to God
And he studied God's word.
Still there were no crops.
Had his prayers gone unheard?

He looked up at God
And said, "What should I do?
I have studied and read
And sang praises to you."

God spoke the answer
To the question he had asked.
"What have you done
To accomplish this task?"

The farmer replied,
"Lord, I trusted in you.
I believed for my faith
You would give me my due."

Then God spoke
And gave revelation.
"You have to create
For me to bless your creation."

"I have provided your fields
And your seed to sow.
You need to plow and to plant
If you want crops to grow."

"It's true you've been faithful
In worship and in praise,
But faith without works
Is like years without days."

"When you are idle
And have no labor to show,
The harvest received
Reflects what you sow."

"You're defined as a farmer
By the work of your hand,
By sowing the seed,
And working the land."

"People will know you're a farmer.
They won't have to guess
When the fruit of your labor
Is what I came to bless."

Receiving God's answer,
He sowed his field.
As he worked for the Lord,
His fruit was revealed.

Each tree is recognized
By its own fruit.
Is your life as a Christian
Up for dispute?

If we wait on God
To do everything,
Why does he need us?
What good do we bring?

Prepare for God's work
With study and praise.
Then walk in his love,
And he'll truly amaze.

When we accept Jesus
And work for the Lord,
An eternity in heaven
Will be our reward.

By William C. Scheel II

True Friends Are Like Jesus

We all travel down the road of life,
Meeting friends along the way.
Some pass from our company quickly,
While others decide to stay.

Friends come in all shapes and sizes
From fat, to tall, to thin.
In reality, it's not the looks that count;
It's the person who lies within.

There are friends who like to party
And are always having fun.
And when the party's ended,
You will find that they are gone.

So, what happens when you hurt
And are laden with despair?
You feel you cannot go on
And the pain is too much to bear.

You reach out for your buddies
And find that you're alone.
It seems the party is over
And there is no one left at home.

That is when you discover true friends,
The ones who really care.
When all of your good-time buddies leave,
You will find your friends still there.

They take the time to listen;
They're concerned about how you feel.
It is in times of trouble when you find
Which friendships are truly real.

Never forget that having friends
Requires friendship too.
You need to care and be there,
Just like they were with you.

So next time a friend is in trouble,
Stop and think before you walk away.
And never let yourself forget
That true friends are here to stay.

God gave me these words
When I first wrote this poem,
But now I understand
That we are never alone.

There is one true friend we have
Who is always there.
No matter how much we hurt,
He will take the time to care.

He is the shining example
Of what it means to be a friend.
No matter the situation,
He will be there till the end.

You have probably heard his name
He is Jesus, Son of God.
And the selfless love he gives
To the world seems very odd.

Our human nature tells us
That our first priority
Should be to make sure
That we take care of I and me.

Jesus will tell us all,
That priority's upside down.
Only when we are last
Can we then wear the crown.

"What is this crown?" you ask.
It's the Crown of Victory.
The victory is over fear,
Which when won, will set us free.

When we face life's worst trials,
We feel so very alone.
All have to do is call Jesus.
We don't even need a phone

He is waiting there to listen.
It doesn't matter when you call.
No matter what the problems are,
He is glad to take them all.

All he asks us in return
Is to walk in love and joy,
And to be a light for goodness
That the world cannot destroy.

Live your life for others
And to be the friend that's there.
When those around us hurt,
He wants us to show we care.

By doing this, he heals us;
And this is just the start.
As we grow in faith and trust,
We gain peace of the heart.

So, stop a second and think about
The treasures that you gather.
Do they bring you peace and joy
Or are they as reliable as the weather?

And if the world has left you empty,
Alone and full of pain,
And if you are drowning in despair,
Just call out his name.

He is waiting for your call.
You don't have to be afraid.
And when you get to know him,
A lifelong friendship will be made.

Jesus is the true friend
That all of us can be.
All we have to do is love him
And obey him faithfully.

The world will stare in wonder
When we are that true friend.
And the peace and joy that fills us
Through Jesus will transcend.

By William C. Scheel II

Reflections

Be God's Beacon

God illuminates the world
To help us find our way.
God's gifts of truth and love
Are like the light of day.

The devil brings the night,
Where doubt and fear abide.
He blacks out truth and love
And gives sin a place to hide.

God, through his love and grace,
Has allowed each of us to choose
To hide in sin and darkness
Or to be a beacon he can use.

Do your desires of the flesh
Hide God's precious light?
Are you feeling lost and alone
And hidden from God's sight?

God's love and comfort await you.
Take his word into your heart.
When you embrace his son, Jesus,
You get a brand-new start.

God said, "Let light shine out of darkness."
And Jesus said, "I am the light of the world."
As you accept Jesus as your savior,
Your new life will be unfurled.

Our salvation is assured,
And the devil's kingdom we will weaken
As we walk with Jesus daily
And choose to be God's beacon.

By William C. Scheel II

Expedience is Obedience

Each of us face tough choices
That will test our heart and mind.
Our priorities when we face them
Is how our character's defined.

When life's trials present themselves
And it's time for us to choose,
Is the integrity of the decision we make
Based on what we can lose?

Expedience is a means to an end,
Especially one that's convenient.
It could possibly be improper too,
When our morality's too lenient.

It seems easy to do the expedient thing
When our well-being is at stake.
But are the decisions that are selfish
Worth the risk we take?

Are you willing to do anything
To make sure you come out on top
By ignoring promises to others
And doing what you'd promised to stop?

The lie you told, the gain you took,
The decision without much thought,
These are all things you'd done before.
But it's different when you get caught.

As a dog returns to his vomit,
So a fool repeats his folly.
Now your expedient lack of wisdom
Has left you melancholy.

If only you had done what's right,
You wouldn't be in this situation.
It worked before, but not this time.
Now you're trapped in tribulation.

There is a different path to take
When it's time to make that choice.
Don't be hasty or self-serving.
Take the time to hear God's voice.

Obedience is compliance to order or law
Or submission to another's authority.
When we submit and obey God's law,
Then we become God's priority.

If you are willing and obedient,
You will eat the best from the land.
But if you resist and rebel,
You will be devoured by God's hand.

A righteous man utters wisdom,
And his tongue speaks what is just.
We are blessed when we honor God,
And our obedience is a must.

If this all sounds confusing
And you're not sure what to do,
God has a salvation plan
That he designed just for you.

The shining example of obedience
Is God's son, Jesus's, life.
He could have made the expedient choice
To avoid his pain and strife.

He not only suffered traumatically,
But also died an innocent death.
He became God's sacrificial lamb
And was obedient till his last breath.

He selflessly obeyed God's plan
To wash away our sin.
And through our obedience to God,
We can be forgiven for who we've been.

So, no matter what has happened,
Just know you control your fate.
Now's the time to call on Jesus.
It can be disastrous if you wait.

In life you can never know
The coming of death's door.
If death takes you by surprise,
What will your eternity hold in store?

So, when you stand before the Lord
On that final judgment day.
Do you want to be standing there all alone
And not knowing what to say?

Or do you want the Son of God
Standing there with you?
Through Jesus, all our sins
Are hidden from God's view.

When you claim your victory in Jesus.
You can start your life anew.
And through his grace and forgiveness,
He will do a work in you.

You will overcome the trouble
That sinful expedience brings.
And a peace and joy will fill you
As you cast down worldly things.

Live your life as Jesus did.
Don't settle for worldly expedience.
The way to eternal salvation
Is through your joyful obedience.

By William C. Scheel II

Life is a Fork in the Road

Life is a road for each of us,
Leading to parts unknown.
Some make the journey with others,
While some make it alone.

From shortly after the time we're born,
We start learning wrong from right.
We learn when we should walk away
And when we should stand and fight.

We learn about the love of God,
And we learn the things of man.
We start to discover love and faith
and struggle the best we can.

All the things that we learn
Become the values we hold.
Some of us become timid,
While others of us are bold.

The values we develop
Become our light that guides.
And the choices that we make
Ultimately shape our lives.

God has granted to all of us
The right to choose our way.
And the sum total of our decisions
Will define our judgment day.

Just as life is a road,
Each choice becomes a fork.
The results can leave us on solid ground
Or bobbing like a cork.

When driving down a road
And finding you are lost,
You can retrace your path,
And time is the only cost.

With life there is no turning back
Once you have made the turn.
No matter what the lesson is,
Did you take the time to learn?

Do you remember the first time
Your life was shaped by choice?
It didn't seem big at the time;
You just heard your inner voice.

Looking back upon that choice,
Do you wonder where you'd be?
Who's voice made the choice
For your responsibility?

Did you ever question that voice
About mistakes you've made?
Did your decision bring you peace
Or leave you lonely and afraid?

Do you feel unable to carry on,
Hopelessly lost and alone?
Has life in the world left you empty?
Are you searching for your home?

Well, my friend, I have some news
That can change that inner voice.
It is a road map to total joy
That involves a simple choice.

What would you do if I told you
that you are just one turn away
from finding the road to victory
on that final judgment day?

It doesn't matter where you traveled
Or even the things you've done.
You can count it all to joy
When you choose Jesus as the One.

He becomes the voice to guide you
Through the trouble and despair.
You'll never be alone again,
Because he is always there.

And when you finally find him
And make him your guiding light,
You'll be on that narrow road
And know the fork that's right.

But even if you falter,
As all us humans do,
He will be there in forgiveness
With his arms holding you.

And when you stand before the Father,
There will be no need for shame,
Because all our sins are paid for
By Jesus's precious name.

By William C. Scheel II

Mind and Heart Discovered

There are two things that guide us
Through our lives each day.
Both contribute to who we are
And work to guide our way.

Our minds are constantly analyzing
All the things we do.
They record all we see
And shape our point of view.

Our hearts bring us feelings
Of every shape and kind.
And for each record our minds have,
There is a feeling we can find.

Although they work hand in hand
Each and every day.
There are times that one says go
And the other tells us stay.

In these times of indecision
It's so hard to do what's right,
Because the two things we rely on
Just seem to want to fight.

Your heart says, "Do what you feel you need."
Your mind says, "No, that's wrong."
Your mind says, "Do what is right."
But your heart says, "The hurt's too strong."

Your mind tries to think clearly,
But it is drowning in despair.
Your heart has so many questions,
But your mind just isn't there.

Usually too late they find out
That all these things they do
Make things so much worse
For the place they live in you.

They try to trick each other
And try to ease the pain.
But every time they do,
It always seems in vain.

I don't know all the answers,
And sometimes I feel pain.
Sometimes I don't know what to do
And try too hard in vain.

I hope the people whom I love
Will try to really see
That some of these things I do
Are from the turmoil inside of me.

I believe there is a remedy
To this turmoil deep inside.
We have to turn and face it.
We cannot run and hide.

We have to be the very best
We know that we can be.
We have to believe in who we are
If we are ever to be free.

So, inside I am going to try
With every thing I do
To make both my mind and heart
To love and understand too.

It's years later now
Since I first wrote this poem.
The Lord has now entered my life
And made my heart his home.

The wisdom of God's word
has shown to me God's plan.
When I let Jesus in my heart,
I became a better man.

I discovered there is an order
To this internal fight.
Your heart is meant to lead,
Your mind to do what's right.

When you're on your own,
A door closes off your mind.
The tribulation consumes us
And our joy is left behind.

But now when a conflict comes,
I don't worry any more.
Jesus is the key
To open up that door.

He takes on all our burdens
And calms our every fear.
A peace comes to our spirits
When we draw Jesus near.

Our mind and heart united,
We're never alone again.
Peace and joy will fill us
When we let Jesus in.

So if you're feeling empty
And ready for a new start,
Make Jesus lord and master
Over your mind and your heart.

By William C. Scheel II

The first part of this poem was completed on March 21, 1989. It was not truly finished until February 10, 2011. The poem was revised again on April 20, 2011.

The "I" in the Storm

Everyone in this world
experiences joy and strife.
It's how we deal with both
That truly defines our life.

As the storm of strife attacks us,
Do we react in fear?
Or do we just joyfully smile
And know the Lord is near.

How many times in our life
Is it a storm that we create?
When life's pressure comes to bear
And we just can't relate.

We think: How can someone
do this awful thing to me?
I will get my revenge,
Just you wait and see.

Why do they have so much?
I deserve much more.
I'm offended by your words;
They have hurt me to the core.

Why are they so pretty,
while I'm so short and fat?
Why are they well when I am sick?
How can I live with that?

Does there seem a central theme
to this storm of misery?
How much of our anger and suffering
Comes from "I" and "me"?

The swirling storm inside your mind
comes from your own fear.
Anger, pride, and despair
Are the enemy's lies we hear.

If we listen very closely
When our pain is at its worst,
It centers around "I" and "me"
and putting ourselves first.

God, in his infinite wisdom,
Has a better plan for our life.
By casting down all of our fear,
we can overcome the strife.

We need to remove "I" and "me"
From the center of the storm.
We need to replace it with his love
And make this our new norm.

God gives us all the answers.
All we have to do is look.
It is there for us to read
in God's life-instruction book.

God tells us he is first,
then all others; we are last.
He says to live in love and forgiveness
And not dwell on our past.

God's desire for each of us
Is to be his shining light.
To walk upright, to be honest,
And to always do what's right.

And as the world surrounds us
With trouble and despair,
We're at peace in the eye of the storm,
Because God is always there.

By William C. Scheel II

Section III:
Terri's Poetry

Smile

Smile, smile.
Bring a smile to your face.
Don't frown on your world,
Lest I need embrace.

I want you; I love you.
Compassion is ours.
Speak not the mundane,
Lewd guilt or for-shame's.

We speak of love for each other,
and for our Lord.
We make known our admiration,
And kiss with his words.

Smile, my love, long to do our best
When to have and to hold are put to the test.
Frown so little, and smile so much more.
Our hearts and spirits with the winds can soar.

Through heartache and turmoil,
There's Christ, God's son.
His blood shed at Calvary
Makes our victory won.

By Terri Jones-Scheel

Set Free

Now in my heart, my lord has his place.
Overwhelmed Is my soul by his love and his grace.
So practice will I his ways, which are right.
Guided by his spirit, I will walk in his light,
Fearing . . . not even the night.

Praise and all glory be to God on high,
For his mercy and forgiveness have given truth, not lie.
In these days to come, Christ will strengthen me,
That my words and actions will glorify thee.

Here now, in his joy
And hope, which sets me free,
I will please the Lord of Life,
His care I will never leave.

By Terri Jones-Scheel

When You Love Someone

When you love someone,
You live to see them smile.
When you love someone,
You'd walk with them the mile.

When you love someone,
You'd do what you must do
To ensure deeper love that will
Surely get you through.

When you love someone,
You will give the best of you.
When you love someone,
Each day feels brand-new.

When you love someone,
You can share their hopes and tears.
When you love someone,
You'll promise to be near.

When you love someone,
You pray for the will to stand.
When you love someone,
You'll see them strong again.

When you love someone. . . .

By Terri Jones-Scheel

River of Love

You see a river runnin' dry?
But not my freedom; that keeps me nigh.
I love the nature this freedom brings.
My love for it is everything.

God gives me freedom, grants it with my tears.
God, I love for you;
You know I do,
Because you're true and sincere!

By Terri Jones-Scheel

Conclusion

Bill Scheel died on March 8, 2012, at the age of fifty-seven. He was born in Houston, Texas, and it was there that he sowed the seeds that bore the fruit of his cherished life. This collection of poetry represents his complete works. He was inspired by those around him, and he was, in turn, inspiring to them. He will be greatly missed by all who knew him.

www.ingramcontent.com/pod-product-compliance
Lightning Source LLC
Chambersburg PA
CBHW071009040426

42443CB00007B/733